Mindfulness for everyday people

EVERYDAY MINDFULNESS IN PRACTICE

Simple and practical ways for everyday mindfulness

ANNA FOX

Copyright © 2017 Anna Fox

All rights reserved. No part of this publication may be reproduced, distributed, or transmitted in any form or by any means, including photocopying, recording, or other electronic or mechanical methods, without written permission from the publisher.

ISBN: 9781549630156

www.everyday-seekers.com

For all Everyday Seekers.

Free download

Just to say thank you for purchasing my book, I would like to give you the Gratitude Journal mentioned in this book for FREE.

Get your FREE copy of "Gratitude Journal – 365 days of gratitude, inspiring quotes and photographs" here:

download.everyday-seekers.com

CONTENTS

INTRODUCTION	1
What is mindfulness?	1
Benefits of mindfulness	5
Basic principles of mindfulness	6
CHAPTER 1: EVERYDAY MINDFULNESS IN PRACTICE	9
CHAPTER 2: MINDFUL MORNING	11
Mindful breathing	12
Mindful meditation	14
Sun Salutation	16
CHAPTER 3: MINDFUL DAY	21
Mindful work	21
Mindful eating	24
Mindful communication	27
CHAPTER 4: MINDFUL EVENING	31
Mindful walking	32
Gratitude	35
Body scanning	38
CONCLUSION	41
ABOUT THE AUTHOR	43

INTRODUCTION

What is mindfulness?

According to the Oxford Dictionary's definition, mindfulness is the quality or state of being conscious or aware of something, a mental state achieved by focusing one's awareness on the present moment, while calmly acknowledging and accepting one's feelings, thoughts and bodily sensations.

Mindfulness is more than just a practice, more than meditation and more than a stress reduction program. Mindfulness is a way of living and a way of being.

You can practice mindfulness in a way that you become aware and present in everyday life, in everyday experiences, on a moment to moment basis and this awareness will become a natural way of expressing yourself and perceiving life. In a way, mindfulness is a new skill that you need to learn and by practicing it, you are making it a part of your being. Eventually, mindfulness will become a natural part of you, effortlessly and organically. It will become a way of being.

Mindfulness is a way of perceiving the world. It includes living in the moment, being in the now, but also, it is the way you look at your emotions, thoughts, events that are happening to you, your circumstances and the world around you. Mindfulness includes viewing all of those things from a place of non-judgment, acceptance and neutrality.

The goal is to perceive all events as neutral and just experience them without attaching any labels and meaning to them. The goal is to accept all of your expressions as they come and let them unfold naturally without putting any attachment on them.

Usually, people's suffering and pain comes more from their story and interpretation of some event, some emotion or thought, than from the event itself.

Maybe you were just leaving your house on your way to work and you saw your neighbor in his yard. Maybe you said hello but he did not respond. Maybe you waited for him to greet you first but that did not happen. Now, on your way to work you are creating a whole story around that event. You are thinking about how rude he was that and you cannot believe that you lived next door to that guy for years and he pretends that you are invisible. He clearly saw you. Then you go on to add all kinds of adjectives. After a while, you come to the conclusion that you will not greet him anymore unless he does it first. You arrive at your work all grumpy, angry and, altogether, not in the mood for anything. Your day started in a negative way and it will possibly continue that way until something bigger catches your mind in a new loop.

In reality, your neighbor maybe did not have his glasses on at the moment you passed his yard and he really did not see you. Or maybe he was wrapped up in his thoughts because his mother is in a hospital and he is really worried about her. But even if he really did see you and did not want to greet you, so what?

If you look at this situation from a place of mindfulness, you would greet your neighbor, he would not greet you back, you would shrug your shoulders and go on about your day without that whole story. You would maybe think: "I hope everything is all right with him." Maybe you would yell louder: "Good morning!" so he could hear you and greet you back. However, whatever happens, you would not think twice about it. Or, if you would, you would consciously let go of those thoughts because your peace is more important than some story that probably is not even true.

This was a simple example but it illustrates how your thoughts create your reality. How you create your reality and how you have the power to choose. You can choose serenity and peace of mind – a mindfulness approach, or you can ruin your whole day.

Mindfulness is not about removing your thoughts or preventing your feelings to appear. It is about observing them from a detached place, it is about not judging them but about acknowledging their presence and just letting them go.

With this practice, in time, your thoughts will appear less and less, stories you have will become shorter and shorter and your view on life and your experiences will become more positive.

Imagine applying that approach of just observing everything without adding any story to it. Imagine the peace and serenity that you would feel, that surrender to the flow of life.

Is that not worth trying?

"Mindfulness is the aware, balanced acceptance of the present experience. It isn't more complicated than that. It is opening to or receiving the present moment, pleasant or unpleasant, just as it is, without either clinging to it or rejecting it."
~ *Sylvia Boorstein*

Benefits of mindfulness

Mindfulness is all about the mind, body, and spirit. It can benefit you in all of these areas. Although mindfulness is not a religious practice, it can be spiritual.

The practice of mindfulness can help you be more engaged in your activities, be more present in everyday life and everyday experiences, have better and deeper connections with other people, improve your relationships, and help you focus. It can decrease anxiety, worry, fear, concerns, low self-esteem, and emotional reactivity. It can increase empathy and compassion. It can deepen your connection with yourself and your needs, wants, and desires. It can improve your whole well-being and quality of life.

Also, mindfulness can improve your physical health by reducing stress, lowering your blood pressure, alleviating gastrointestinal difficulties, improving sleep, and boosting your working memory.

It can improve your mental health by helping you with depression, eating disorders, addictions, anxiety disorders, and obsessive-compulsive disorder.

People are holistic beings and everything is connected and intertwined – mind, body, and spirit – so when you affect one part, you are affecting all of them. Mindfulness can offer that holistic approach to life, to health, and to your well-being.

> "When your attention moves into the Now, there is an alertness. It is as if you were waking up from a dream, the dream of thought, the dream of past and future. Such clarity, such simplicity. No room for problem-making. Just this moment as it is."
> ~ Eckhart Tolle

Basic principles of mindfulness

Detachment – people often get attached to feelings, emotions, and thoughts. They tend to replay pleasurable experiences over and over again, but also tend to dwell on unpleasant experiences. By letting go (not forgetting but releasing attachment) of everything that comes your way, you remain unstuck, in the flow of life.

Being in the now – by letting go, you are able to focus on the present moment, live in the now, and that is the only moment that exists. The past is behind you and you cannot change it, you can just learn from it, and the future is yet to come and the only place from which you can influence its outcome is in the present.

Non-judgment – people tend to attach labels to their experiences and judge them as good or bad and view their emotions as positive or negative. One of the mindfulness principles is to not judge anything or add your story to it but observe things as they are.

Openness – this means letting go of your rigid view of the world, thinking that your way is the only way, letting go of thought patterns and beliefs and being open to everything, being open to new experiences, other perspectives, and other points of view.

Acceptance – acceptance means to stop trying to change your reality by force or acting like a victim. With acceptance, you are aware that you can change your reality only by taking responsibility for your life and your actions. By acceptance, you are both trusting and surrendering to life and taking conscious actions to make things happen.

~

Mindfulness is a very simple and powerful practice but it is not always easy.

When you deal with minor events that do not have significant meaning to you then you can accept, detach and let go easier. However, some emotions, thoughts, and beliefs go deep, often deep into the childhood, and observing them without engaging is not easy. In those moments, kindness, love, and non-judgment are very important, as are patience and persistence. With time and practice, even those deep beliefs can be released for good.

Often times, people tend to suppress their emotions and thoughts because they do not want to feel that discomfort, they think that the pain is unbearable and they will not be able to deal with it. However, the truth is the total opposite. The longer you suppress something, the longer that something has the power over you, the longer it poisons you from the inside, and the longer it stays.

You are not your emotions, you are not your thoughts. You are the one behind them, you are the one observing them. If you approach them from that detached place, from the place of non-judgment, if you just observe them to see what happens, how they look, what color they are, how they taste, and what shape they have, then you will see that they have no power over you. You will see through them, you will see the space behind them, they will just dissolve and all that will be left is you as an observer. From that place, answers and solutions to your struggles will come.

"The best way to capture moments is to pay attention. This is how we cultivate mindfulness. Mindfulness means being awake. It means knowing what you are doing."
~ Jon Kabat-Zinn

CHAPTER 1:
EVERYDAY MINDFULNESS IN PRACTICE

How to be mindful every day while dealing with everyday stuff?

The beautiful thing about mindfulness is that everything can become mindfulness practice – literally everything. Whatever you do mindfully, with presence and an awareness of what you are doing, you are practicing mindfulness. This can be as simple as drinking your tea, washing your dishes, petting your cat. If you are fully in the moment and aware of the cup you are holding and the warmth you are feeling on your skin, and if you are present and observing every sip of tea that you take and how it tastes in your mouth, you are practicing mindfulness.

That said, there are also some simple ways and techniques that you can apply in your life throughout the day that can help you with your mindfulness practice.

I like to say that I am not a life coach, psychologist or some special person with some secret knowledge. I am just a regular everyday person and I have spent a lot of years of my life seeking the answers on how to be my best self and live my best life - a mindful life. Everything I share with you is my personal experience and practices that I tried and that worked for me.

We will cover several morning, day and evening mindful practices:

Mindful morning:
- Mindful breathing
- Mindful meditation
- Sun Salutation

Mindful day:
- Mindful work
- Mindful eating
- Mindful communication

Mindful evening:
- Mindful walking
- Gratitude
- Body scanning

CHAPTER 2:
MINDFUL MORNING

You can start your mindfulness practice from the moment you wake up. I would encourage you to do that because the way you start your morning will reflect through the rest of your day.

You can develop a morning routine that best suits you. Try to do it every day for a week or two and see how you feel, observe what is changing in your inner and outer world. If you need to, alter it according to your lifestyle and preferences. After you see the results and benefits it brings, this will become a positive habit that you will not want to change.

Mindful breathing

The first simple thing you can do in the morning is focus on your breathing. You breathe anyway so this is not something new or complicated or something that requires a big effort. However, mindful breathing or intentional breathing requires your presence in every breath. It requires for you to focus on your breath and observe it.

You can do this before you even get out of bed but if you feel more comfortable, you can sit upright.

First, bring your attention to your breath. Breathe in and out, in and out and in and out some more. Just let yourself breathe as you normally do. Do not try to slow your breath or speed it up. Let it be natural and just observe it without any judgment or story about it. There is no wrong way of doing this. If those kinds of thoughts come up, just let them pass without engaging with them.

Observe your breath and how it flows through your body – your nose, chest, and abdomen.

You will probably notice that with every breath you get more and more relaxed and more and more peaceful.

After a few breaths, set your intention on your abdomen, you can even place your hand there to help you focus. Start taking deeper breaths through your nose and fill your whole lungs and abdomen. Hold your breath for a few moments or however long it feels comfortable to you, and then slowly exhale through your mouth. If you feel up to it, you can also add some sound when exhaling, such as "Ahhh" or "Ommm".

If you find it difficult to focus on your breathing and your mind becomes overactive, you can attach your breath to a simple word or a mantra. This can be as simple as "In" or "Inhale" when you breathe in and "Out" or "Exhale" when you breathe out. This can help your brain to calm and focus easier.

Do this for however long it feels comfortable. Maybe you can set a timer for 3 or 5 minutes or you can count your breaths.

~

This is something you can do at any time and any place throughout the day but by doing this first thing in the morning, you will start your day in a calm place, more relaxed, peaceful and stress-free. You will also fill your body and your brain with more oxygen.

Over time, you will notice that you are breathing more fully and deeply most of the time and this will have long-term positive effects on your body, mind and spirit.

"Breathing in, I calm body and mind. Breathing out, I smile. Dwelling in the present moment I know this is the only moment."
~ Thich Nhat Hanh

Mindful meditation

When you finish your mindful breathing exercise, you can from there just slip into the meditation.

You can return to your normal breathing and observe it. Again, just follow your breath as it goes in and out. You can then expand your awareness to your whole body. Observe how you feel, start from the top of your head and proceed down to your feet. If any part of your body feels tight, just consciously relax it. Release all of the tension from your body.

There are many ways that you can meditate and you should find the one that feels best for you.

If you want, after relaxing your body, you can return to your breath and just observe it. When thoughts appear, just let them go, let them pass through you like they are clouds and you are the sky. If you engage with them, do not judge or blame yourself, just gently return to your breath again.

Thoughts will not disappear, that is not the point of meditation. The point is to observe them and remain neutral. This is something that will happen with time and practice and it is nothing that you need to force.

If you like, you can again add some simple word or mantra to your breathing to help your mind stay calmer. You maybe want to try Hawaiian practice of Ho'oponopono in your meditation by simply using "Thank you" or "I love you" as your mantra.

Maybe you wish to add relaxing music to your

meditation, binaural beats or different healing frequencies such as 432 or 528 Hz. Another great way are guided meditations. You can find some amazing free meditations on YouTube.

One example is the YouTube channel "The Honest Guys", where you can find free high-quality guided meditations for every occasion. If they do not resonate with you, try to find someone that does, or simply practice breath meditation.

If you like, you can again set the timer for 5 or 10 minutes or you can simply let your inner guidance let you know when you have had enough.

~

Benefits of meditation are incredible. To name a few, meditation can reduce stress and anxiety, improve focus and concentration, bring calmness, happiness, and acceptance, increase your health, quality of life and well-being.

Try different ways of meditating so you can find what best works for you.

"Life is a mystery – mystery of beauty, bliss and divinity. Meditation is the art of unfolding that mystery."
~ Amit Ray

Sun Salutation

The Sun Salutation, or Surya Namaskar, is a yogic technique that contains a series of postures, or asanas, that are practiced in a consecutive sequence. There is a whole science behind this ancient technique, as it is behind yoga in general, but we will not go into that now.

The Sun Salutation can be a warm up for a yoga routine but it can also be practiced on its own and this is one more morning mindfulness technique that I recommend. Practiced on its own, this is a complete exercise that engages every part of the body, energizes it and helps start the day in a mindful, aware and positive way.

Do it at a pace you feel comfortable and do not worry about doing it perfectly. There is no need to force anything. You can repeat the sequence as many times as it feels good for you.

Yoga is a great mindfulness practice because it can help you be in the moment, in the movement, and in the breath. As you move through the postures, try to observe your inhales and exhales and feel your body's movements.

- Start by standing upright with your feet together and balancing your weight equally on both feet. Relax your shoulders and expand your chest. As you inhale, lift both of your arms up from the sides. As you exhale, bring your palms together in front of the chest in a prayer position.
- As you inhale, lift your arms up and back, keeping the biceps close to the ears. Try to stretch your whole body up, from the heels to the tips of the fingers.
- As you exhale, bend forward at the waist, slightly soften your knees and fold forward with your hands down to the floor, beside your feet.
- As you inhale, flat your back and lengthen the spine with your hands on the fingertips on the floor in front of you.
- As you exhale, push your right leg as far back as possible, put your knee to the floor and look up. If you feel more advanced, you can also jump back, directly into the next posture with both of your feet (as explained in the video below).
- As you inhale, plant the palms and put your left leg back and bring the whole body in a straight line.
- As you exhale, bring your knees to the floor, slightly take your hips back, slide forward, put your chest and chin on the floor.
- As you inhale, roll forward and upwards, keep your elbows bent and shoulders away from the ears. Keep the back of your neck long and look up.
- As you exhale, ground your hands and feet into

the floor, lift the hips up and put your chest downwards. Take a few deep breaths.
- As you inhale, put your right foot forward in between your hands, left knee down to the floor and look up. If you feel more advanced, you can jump forward, directly into the next posture with both of your feet (as explained in the video below).
- As you exhale, put your left foot forward to join the right. Keep your palms on the floor.
- As you inhale, roll the spine up, put your hands up and bend backward a little bit.
- As you exhale, straighten your body and put your palms together in front of the chest in a prayer position. Relax and observe the sensations in your body.

You can search YouTube for visual guidance. I recommend a video from "Yoga by Candace" – "For Beginners - Sun Salutation A - Each yoga pose explained" because every Sun Salutation posture is shown in slow motion, is well explained and everything is easy to understand.

~

When done regularly, Surya Namaskar can help your nervous and digestive system, improve lung function and blood circulation, correct hormonal imbalances, help with weight loss, strengthen muscles and joints and maintain overall health. Every part of the body can benefit from this practice.

The Sun Salutation is one more way to boost your body, mind, and spirit.

"Yoga does not remove us from the reality or responsibilities of everyday life but rather places our feet firmly and resolutely in the practical ground of experience. We don't transcend our lives; we return to the life we left behind in the hopes of something better."
~ *Donna Farhi*

CHAPTER 3: MINDFUL DAY

After the morning routine, when you go about your day, it is easy to get lost in everyday tasks. Everyone has a million things to do throughout the day but if you consciously practice mindfulness, you can be aware and present in anything you do. Even more so, you can do your tasks with more ease, focus, and efficiency.

Mindful work

When you practice mindfulness, your work can become a perfect place for that.
No matter what you do and what your job is, you can put your focus on the present moment and the

task that is in front of you. This takes a little bit of practice, but with time, it gets easier and easier.

Observe your hands on the keyboard, or the object they are holding, hear the ticking of the clock, or birds outside. Feel the chair you are sitting on. Maybe you are working in nature. Observe the trees, feel the breeze on your skin, the sun on your face. Go to your breath again. Become aware of your thoughts about the job you are doing. Observe your thoughts that are not related to the job you are doing. Observe how you can do the job without even thinking about it. Notice when you go on autopilot and gently return to yourself, to the present moment.

It is amazing when you realize that most of the time you are not even here, you are not in your body. You are miles away, thinking about other places, thinking about your past or your future, but your body still works without being told.

Your heart still pumps blood and brings oxygen and nutrients to the organs and tissues of your body. Your lungs still expand and contract twelve to twenty times per minute so you can breathe. Your body still produces 25 million new cells each second. All of that while you are thinking about your grocery list and what you need to buy on your way home from work.

Amazing is the fact that you are also working while thinking about your grocery list and you are not even present most of the time. Imagine how much more you could accomplish if you are actually present and aware of what you are doing.

~

Mindful work is mindfulness in practice, in everyday life and everyday tasks. Mindfulness is not something that only Buddhist monks can practice isolated from the world and people. Mindfulness is something that everyday people, regardless of their circumstances, can practice in each and every moment.

The most important thing is to keep returning to yourself, to your body, to the present moment. At first, this will maybe happen once or twice in an hour, when you realize that your mind and your thoughts are caught up in that loop again, in some story that is playing in your head, a story that you became a part of without even realizing it.

In time, you will realize that you are more and more present, more and more here and now. You will notice that your mind is more peaceful and that you are more focused on where you are and what you are doing.

"We're so busy watching out for what's just ahead of us that we don't take the time to enjoy where we are."
~ *Bill Watterson*

Mindful eating

The same principles can be applied to eating. People often eat without even tasting the food. They eat on their feet or are distracted by the TV or newspapers. They are not aware when they are really hungry or what their bodies need and want to eat.

For mindful eating, all it takes is a bit of awareness.

Mindful eating means to pay attention to the food you are eating, before and during your meal.

When you feel hunger, pay attention to your body. Observe how it feels. Observe where you feel hunger. Is your body really hungry or is your mind the one that is craving food? On a scale from 1 to 10, how hungry are you? We are often actually thirsty when we think that we are hungry. Did you drink enough water today?

If you indeed feel physical hunger, observe what your body craves. Which food do you need? It may take a little bit of practice to be able to distinguish the difference between your body's actual needs and your mind's cravings. If you pay attention, your body will let you know what food you need, what is maybe missing in your organism and what food you need to eat more or less.

After you identify what food you want to eat and when you sit down to eat it, try to do it in a peaceful place. When you are eating mindfully, this means that you are paying attention to the food. You can even make it a little ritual of yours.

You do not want distractions such as TV or newspapers, because when you are trying to do two things at the same time, you are actually not able to enjoy and be present with either of them, and you cannot be fully aware of your body and its signals.

Start by observing the food in front of you. Notice the colors, smells, and texture. Then take a bite and really taste it in your mouth. Notice how it feels and how it tastes. Maybe you will notice that it tastes different than you remember because this is the first time you are eating this food consciously. Maybe it is even tastier than you thought or maybe you do not like it as much. When you are eating this way, you can enjoy your food much more.

Pay attention to your body and your stomach. Is it full? Have you had enough to eat? Do you need more? There is no need to eat after you are full. People are mostly raised to not throw food and to eat everything that is on their plate, but if that means that you will overeat and feel discomfort and pain afterward, then this is a belief that no longer serves you. You can always eat the rest of the food later but, let's be honest, no matter if you eat the food or throw it away, it turns to waste. In time, you may even notice that you need smaller meals and you will learn to prepare them that way.

When you are finished, sit for a moment or two and let yourself enjoy the fullness. Let the food settle for a while and give your body time to digest it.

Also, observe your thoughts around the food. If

you keep counting your calories or combining your food, if you keep telling yourself that you eat too much or that you need to lose weight, be gentle with those thoughts and emotions that follow them.

Try to be kind and loving with yourself and not judge anything that shows up. Allow your thoughts to pass through you and let them go. Always gently return to the now moment.

~

Just do your best to incorporate mindful eating into your every meal.

Remember to slow down, pay attention to your body and its signals and needs, do one thing at the time and enjoy your every meal with all your senses.

"Mindful eating is a way to become reacquainted with the guidance of our internal nutritionist."
~ Jan Chozen Bays

Mindful communication

By practicing mindfulness, you can deepen your relationships.

People are often somewhere else in their mind and not with the person they are talking to. More often than not, while the other person is talking, they are thinking about what they are going to say next, or they are checking their phone, and they are not fully present in the conversation.

When you bring your awareness in the conversation and when you are fully present, you can actually hear what the other person is saying to you. You can then engage and contribute to the conversation in a meaningful and deeper way. Try to be fully open to the other person and his or her words and perspective and allow it to be different to yours. Observe it openly and maybe you will notice something that will broaden your beliefs and opinions.

Try to fully listen and pay attention to the conversation. Observe the other person, their body language, and the energy behind their words. People are not talking to each other just with words. When you are aware and present in the moment, you will be able to notice that subtle messages beyond the words.

When you are talking, also be present in the moment. The interesting thing is that when you step out of that mind loop of thinking and storytelling, your conversations can become more fluid, more real and more from the heart. Words will come out of your mouth regardless of the thinking process. When you are practicing mindful conversations, your relationships become mindful and more meaningful.

Another benefit of mindfulness in relationships is that when you are fully present and when you observe your emotions, thoughts, and feelings that appear when you are engaging with someone, you can very quickly notice how someone is resonating with you. You can more easily sense their intentions but, also, you can sense your response to that person and whether you want to spend your time and energy on them or not. You can sense with more ease if a person is toxic or if they are someone who will enrich your life with their presence.

You are also more aware of your core values, needs and wants and can express them to the other person in that moment, rather than having any regrets later. You are becoming more and more authentic in your everyday life.

By being mindful, you can also let go of things with more ease and your emotional reactivity can decrease, so you can resolve conflict and forgive more quickly, or not even hold a grudge about insignificant things. When you are not attaching any additional story to someone's actions, and when you are fully present and can easily see someone's intentions, then your relationship with that person becomes easier.

~

When you are aware of the other person and yourself in the present moment, you can be more understanding, compassionate and emphatic, be more aware of their needs and feelings, and altogether be a better friend, lover or a parent. Through mindfulness, you can connect with people on a much deeper level. Mindfulness can help you have more heart-based relationships.

"Remember that there is only one important time and it is now. The present moment is the only time over which we have dominion. The most important person is always the person with whom you are, who is right before you, for who knows if you will have dealings with any other person in the future? The most important pursuit is making that person, the one standing at your side, happy, for that alone is the pursuit of life."
~ Leo Tolstoy

CHAPTER 4:
MINDFUL EVENING

When you practice mindfulness in the evening, you can let go of your day, leave its tasks behind you, relax fully into the evening and prepare yourself for a good night sleep of rejuvenation. Everything that happened throughout the day is over, it is in the past, and everything that you will need to address tomorrow is in the future and there is no need to worry about that either.

However you like to spend your evening and whatever your evening activities are, always return to the present moment and observe.

There are some simple ways that can help you be mindful in the evening. Of course, you can practice any of the mentioned activities at any time, but in the evening, they can help you let go of your day with more ease. Commit to this practice for a week or two and see how you feel about it and what changes it brings to your life.

Mindful walking

After a long day of sitting in the office, a mindful walk could be just the thing that your body needs. If your job is more physical, you will still benefit from this but maybe you will find other practices more appealing in the evening. However, whatever your job is, a mindful walk, preferably in nature, will help you leave your job behind you for that day and just be here and now, and reconnect with yourself.

If possible, wear something comfortable. If you can, go for a walk in nature, somewhere away from the traffic because this is a great way to connect more with nature. It also makes your walk a more enjoyable experience.

Start your walk at your normal pace, there is no need to rush anywhere. There is also no need for a specific destination as the walk itself is the purpose. Become aware of your body, of your feet touching the ground, of the sounds and smells that surround you, sensations that you feel on your skin, everything that you see around you. Notice your posture, your movements, your breathing. Observe the present moment and everything that is in it.

When you notice that you drifted away into your

mind, observe your thoughts, emotions, and moods without any judgment and without any extra story. Just observe what is happening and gently focus your attention back into your physical body, back to the walking.

If it helps, you can add some words to your breathing, just like in meditation, to replace your mental activity. Maybe "Inhale" and "Exhale" or just a mantra like "Omm" or "Thank you".

Pay attention to your environment; notice what is there. If you are in nature, connect with it, let it heal you, immerse yourself in that pure reviving energy.

Walk for however long it feels comfortable for you, 5, 10, 20, 30 minutes or more if you like.

The benefits of mindful walking are similar to meditation, but walking - physical movement - can have additional benefits to your health and well-being such as relieving arthritis, improving digestion, increasing stamina and strength, reducing the risk of heart disease, stroke, diabetes, preventing dementia, boosting vitamin D, increasing oxygen supply, filling you with energy and boosting your mood.

Mindful walking is a practice - something you will get better at over time. At first, your mind could be overactive and you maybe notice that your autopilot took over and you came home without even realizing it. That is okay, in time, your mind will become quieter.

Whenever you notice that your mind drifted away, just come back to yourself, come back to the here and now, come back to your body. Soon you will notice this more often and more quickly.

The point is to just come back from wherever you went and whenever you realize it. Just come back again and again.

The best thing is that you can practice mindful walking every time you walk.

~

Walking is a simple yet incredibly powerful way that can bring you fully in the present moment and in your body.

This is an active practice and an active form of meditation and a great way to integrate mindfulness into your everyday life.

"In every walk with nature, one receives far more than he seeks."
~ John Muir

Gratitude

The practice of gratitude can bring you into the present moment because you are focusing on what is already here in your life. To be grateful means to focus on the blessings you have in the present moment, no matter how small or big they are. It means becoming fully aware of your life and not taking anything for granted.

Gratitude practice can slowly change your mindset and perspective on life and how you perceive life's situations by shifting your focus.

People who practice gratitude experience more positive emotions, express more compassion and kindness, are more satisfied with life, sleep better and even have stronger immune systems.

Before sleep, go through your day and find 1 or 3 or 5 things you are grateful for. On some days, you will have more to write and on some days, you will have less, and that is perfectly okay. When you actively start looking for things you are grateful for on an everyday basis, more and more will appear.

You can use some pretty notebook or your computer or phone to keep a gratitude journal. Maybe you will take some notes during the day that you will enter in your journal when you notice something you are grateful for. Maybe you will reflect upon your day in the evening and write them all then. Find what works for you. If journaling is not your thing, try to find other ways to express your gratitude.

Things to be grateful for can be big, like the birth of your child, but they can also be, and usually will be, small, like having a meaningful conversation with a friend, eating a delicious lunch or watching a breathtaking sunset. Try to really feel what you write.

Be creative with this if you like. There is no rule that you only need to write lists. Try adding some photographs, tickets, pressed flowers, turn your diary into a scrapbook at times, draw something, add whatever is meaningful for you and represent something you are grateful for.

To help you maintain the practice of gratitude, try to notice different things every day, be as specific as possible so you do not repeat the same phrase over and over again, even if you are grateful for the same thing every day. Avoid making superficial lists. For example, if you are writing about your family try to write about specific situations from that day. If keeping a journal becomes just another chore in your day, try writing it every other day or twice per week - see what works best for you.

When you are writing about what you are grateful for, observe your body, your thoughts, and emotions. Observe how you feel when you think and write about these moments. Observe the pen leaving its trail on the paper, or letters that are appearing on the screen, observe your hands and fingers as you write. Be mindful about the whole process.

~

Even when life is hard, even when it feels unbearable, the practice of gratitude can help you to see that there is always beauty present, that there are always opportunities that are available, and that there is joy in the simple moments. It can help you to see that everything does not need to be perfect for you to be happy, that you can be happy in the little now moments because there will not be an "everything is perfect" moment anyway.

If you go through your day looking for something to be grateful for, something will always show up. Always.

Download your free copy of "Gratitude Journal – 365 days of gratitude, inspiring quotes and photographs" at download.everyday-seekers.com and see how you like it.

"It's a funny thing about life, once you begin to take note of the things you are grateful for, you begin to lose sight of the things that you lack."
~ Germany Kent

Body scanning

Body scanning is a conscious awareness of physical appearance, sensations, and movement in the body. It means observing your body, becoming aware of its different regions and just feeling the sensations in them, without any judgment or story. Like with any mindfulness practice, the point is to just notice, to be in the now with acceptance and openness.

You can do this lying in your bed just before you go to sleep. In fact, you will probably fall asleep with ease with this practice. If you fall asleep during your body scan, that is also okay.

Start by feeling the sensations of your body on the bed, feel your back touching the mattress, feel the warmth of your body, feel the clothes on your skin. Observe how it feels to be lying on the bed.

Bring your attention to your breathing. Notice every breath, every time you inhale and exhale. Observe the rhythm of your breathing, your lungs expanding and contracting, your abdomen moving, and your breath flowing through your body.

Bring your awareness to the top of your head. Notice any sensations or the absence of them. Observe how it feels. Notice how the sensations are changing. If any thoughts appear, do not judge them but notice them and let them go. Return to your body and continue with your scan.

Focus on your face, feel the muscles, feel your

jaw, is there any tension there? Are they relaxed? Just observe without any need to change anything. What sensations are you feeling? What color are they, what shape? If you like, you can breathe in every part of the body you observe. Also, try to wide and narrow your focus. Feel a particular part of your body such as your ear, or expand your focus to your whole head.

Continue to move down the body. Come back to attention each time you notice that your mind has drifted into thinking. Become aware of your thoughts and let them go, let them flow through you without attaching to them, without engaging with them. Be kind and patient with yourself.

If you notice any pain or discomfort, just observe it as neutrally as you can. When you do not avoid these sensations, when you lean into them and let yourself feel them without any additional thoughts and story, you will reduce their power over you. By removing any thoughts attached to these sensations, you are removing a big part of your pain or discomfort. Sometimes thoughts about the pain that you keep repeating to yourself are more painful than the feeling itself.

When you finish your scan, bring your attention back to the whole body and its sensations. Notice your breathing again, the feeling of the clothes on your skin, texture of the sheets. Stay there for several moments and observe.

This can be a 3, 5 or 10-minute scan, or longer if you feel like it. See what works for you.

You can also listen to a guided body scan if you

like. Try a short 5-minute guided body scan from "Yoga by Candace" on YouTube which is a great start – "5 Min Guided Meditation Body Scan".

You can also find longer ones on YouTube. Try several versions and see what feels best for you.

~

With this practice, you will get in touch with your body, release tension and stress from your day and return to the present moment. By doing this practice regularly, you will notice that you are living from your body more and more. Your mind will become quieter with time.

You will also be more connected with your body's signals and sensations and will be able to detect with greater ease what it needs for its optimal health. You will develop more appreciation and gratitude towards your body. This can help you to release unhealthy body image, judgment, and self-criticism.

Through the body scanning practice, you can learn to connect with your body on a much deeper level and love and respect your body more.

> *"The body always leads us home… if we can simply learn to trust sensation and stay with it long enough for it to reveal appropriate action, movement, insight, or feeling."*
> *~ Pat Ogden*

CONCLUSION

Thank you for purchasing *"Mindfulness for everyday people: EVERYDAY MINDFULNESS IN PRACTICE - Simple and practical ways for everyday mindfulness"*!

I hope this book was able to provide you with some inspiration, motivation and practical ways for everyday mindfulness.

Maybe you will just want to try one or two practices mentioned in this book or maybe you will want to create your own morning or evening routine and ritual.

Go for it! Include mindfulness in your everyday life in a way that resonates and works best for you, your body, mind, and spirit.

I wish you all the best on your journey.

Finally, if you enjoyed this book, would you be kind enough to leave an honest review? It would be greatly appreciated!

Thank you and good luck!

ABOUT THE AUTHOR

I am a dreamer, seeker, life passionista, and a much, much more. I am the author of "Mindfulness for everyday people: HOW TO BE YOUR BEST SELF AND LIVE YOUR BEST LIFE – Simple life-changing steps for everyday mindfulness", "Mindfulness for everyday people: EVERYDAY MINDFULNESS IN PRACTICE – Simple and practical ways for everyday mindfulness", and "Gratitude Journal – 365 days of gratitude, inspiring quotes, and photographs".

I am not a life coach or a psychologist, I am not some special person with any secret knowledge. I am just a regular everyday person and I have spent a lot of years of my life seeking the answers on how to be my best self and live my best life – a mindful life. I am trying to improve, grow, and learn. That is something that never ends. I am trying to live authentically every day and I am striving to be the best version of myself and live up to my potentials.

I have read many books and taken many courses to find those answers, but most importantly, I lived through a lot of experiences that made me who I am today and helped me grow and become my best self. I struggled with depression, an eating disorder, health problems, pain from losing my father at the age of 12, a challenging and painful childhood, and finding my purpose and meaning.

I overcame a lot of pain, struggles, obstacles, and setbacks and I can tell you from experience that it can be done. You can come to the other side stronger, wiser, better, and more complete as a person. You can find yourself and your truth through life's hard situations and moments. You can have mindfulness in everyday life.

I'm in love with life and I think it's magical. I'm a big kid and a dreamer. I do what I love, I love what I do, and I don't see it as work.

I love and enjoy reading (anything and everything, from spiritual literature, literary classics, and expert books to SF and romance novels), music (I perceive music very emotionally so I listen to whatever moves me), volunteering (my favorite was therapeutic horseback riding), long walks in the woods with my Labrador, Rose, long conversations with loved ones (if they are combined with long walks then you can't shush me), laughing (especially with loved ones during long conversations combined with long walks), dancing (to 50's, 60's, 70's, 80's rock music, until the early morning hours), good tea (my favorites are Yogi teas, all tastes and types), rain (especially walking in the rain, but it's not bad under a blanket either), snow and snowflakes (and again, there are those walks but also a blanket, especially with a good book or good music and a cup of tea)... and the list goes on.

Connect with me at www.everyday-seekers.com

NOTES

NOTES

NOTES

NOTES

NOTES

NOTES

NOTES

NOTES

Printed in Great Britain
by Amazon